ICNC **SPECIAL REPORT** SERIES

The Pashtun Protection Movement (PTM) in Pakistan

by Qamar Jafri

TABLE OF CONTENTS

Introduction 1

I. War, Grievances, and Choice of Response 2

II. Emergence of the Nonviolent Movement and Its First Actions 6

III. Pragmatic Necessity for Nonviolent Resistance 9

IV. Historical Lessons for the PTM: Bacha Khan,
His Red Shirt Movement, and the Cultural Norm of Nonviolent *Badal* 10

V. PTM Leadership: Diversity of Membership and Women's Participation 14

VI. Movement Strategies and Tactics 18
    A. Disruptive Tactics 18
    B. Communication Strategies 18
    C. Constructive Organizing and Creative Actions 21
    D. Strategic Integration of Civil Resistance with Institutional Efforts 23

VII. State Repression and PTM Strategies to Maintain Nonviolent Discipline 25
    A. Repression and Propaganda Against the PTM 25
    B. PTM Nonviolent Discipline in the Face of Repression 27

VIII. Impacts of the PTM 29

Key Takeaways from the PTM for Successful Nonviolent Resistance 32
    A. Mobilizing Ordinary People 32
    B. Funding Campaigns Locally 32
    C. Engaging Local Elites 32
    D. Working with Faith Leaders 32
    E. Building on Local Civil Resistance Legacies 33
    F. Reinforcing Nonviolent Discipline 33
    G. Inclusion of Women in Leadership Roles 33
    H. Representing Multiple Ethnic Groups 33
    I. Balanced Use of Social Media 34

Appendix I: The Terror Networks, the War on Terror, and Their Effects on Tribal Pashtuns 35

Appendix II: A Note on the Interview Subjects 38

Cited Bibliography 39

Image Credits 41

Acknowledgments 42

Text Boxes, Tables, Figures, and Maps

TEXT BOX 1. **What Are the Tribal Areas?** 3

TEXT BOX 2. **What is the FCR?** 5

TEXT BOX 3. **What is the *Pashtunwali* code?** 13

TABLE 1. **A Comparison of the RSM and the PTM** 11

TABLE 2. **Interviewees for This Study** 38

FIGURE 1. **A Demonstration by the Mehsud Tahafuz Movement** 7

FIGURE 2. **The Newly-Formed PTM Holds a Jalsa in Peshawar** 8

FIGURE 3. **A PTM supporter, Along with His Children, Holds a Frame Containing Photos of Bacha Khan and PTM Leader Manzoor Pashteen** 12

FIGURE 4. **Tweet by PTM Activist Tariq** 15

FIGURE 5. **Tweet by PTM Leader Sanna Ejaz** 16

FIGURE 6. **Manzoor Pashteen Addresses a Gathering to Promote Participation in the Long March to Bannu** 20

FIGURE 7. **A PTM Activist Carries a Bundle of Flyers to Distribute Among the Local Public** 21

FIGURE 8. **Tweet by PTM Leader Mohsin Dawar** 22

FIGURE 9. **Activists Collect Funds at a PTM Jalsa** **23**

FIGURE 10. **Youth Sit on the Roof of a Bus to Travel to a PTM Jalsa** **24**

FIGURE 11. **Tweet by PTM Leader Manzoor Pashteen** **26**

MAP 1. **Locations of PTM Jalsas in 2018–2020** **19**

MAP 2. **The Seven Former FATA Regions on the Pakistan–Afghanistan Border.** **36**

INTRODUCTION

IN A MIDNIGHT RAID in Peshawar on January 27, 2020, Pakistani police arrested human rights activist Manzoor Pashteen, charging him with conspiracy, sedition, and other alleged crimes. When the sun rose, tens of thousands of people took to the streets in protest. Over the past seven years, Pashteen and his peers have built a civil resistance movement focused on Pakistan's human rights abuses against members of the minority Pashtun tribe. As the leader of the Pashtun Tahafuz Movement (PTM),[1] Pashteen has guided the movement in using nonviolent tactics in their struggle. In response to the PTM's momentum and recent gains, the Pakistani state has used physical and administrative repression to suppress the movement and create a counternarrative that plays off of stereotypes of Pashtuns being inherently violent and their territory being overrun with jihadists.

In a region profoundly affected by the US War on Terror, the PTM has integrated tribal traditions and international standards of constitutional justice to catalyze a decidedly nonviolent movement for change—a movement so strong that the state could not ignore it and chose to use violence to counter it.

Building on interviews with movement leaders and campaign participants in the field, this special report answers the following questions:

- How and why did the PTM emerge? Why do the Pakistani Pashtuns engage in nonviolent resistance as part of the PTM?

- What is the PTM leadership and organizational structure and how diverse is its membership?

- What role do women play in the PTM?

- What are nonviolent resistance tactics and strategies that the PTM has adopted to advance Pakistani Pashtuns' civil rights?

- How does the PTM remain nonviolent in the face of state violence?

- What is the impact of the PTM's grassroots organizing and nonviolent resistance?

- What are the key lessons learned from the PTM experience?

---

1   "Tahafuz" translates to English as "Protection." This special report often uses the English rendering of the movement's name—Pashtun Protection Movement—while keeping the most commonly used abbreviation "PTM."

I. War, Grievances, and Choice of Response

The war in Afghanistan has contributed to a volatile situation for the Pashtuns of Pakistan's tribal areas. When the United States invaded Afghanistan following the 9/11 terrorist attacks, many Taliban fighters took refuge in the tribal areas of Pakistan (Wazir 2019).[2] The Taliban used this region as a staging ground for military campaigns in neighboring Afghanistan and for violent attacks against civilians and Pakistan's government (Sayers 2007). Pakistan formed an alliance with the United States against the insurgents and, since then, the Pakistani military, with support from the US, has carried out seven major military operations in the tribal areas, causing enormous collateral damage and instability in the region.[3] Though the web of non-state actors in the regional conflict is complicated, the Pakistani government crudely divides the Taliban branch into two categories: the "Good Taliban" or *Mujahideen*—comprised of Afghans and the Haqqani Network who are considered to be pro-Pakistan—and the "Bad Taliban"—namely the *Tehrik-i-Taliban Pakistan* (TTP) or the "Taliban Movement in Pakistan," considered by the Pakistani government to be an enemy.

Pashtuns of the tribal areas became victims of the conflict in four distinct ways. First, they suffered directly from the war. Strict war-time curfews prevented their access to food, water, and healthcare. Indiscriminate bombings, airstrikes, and firings into civilian crowds have contributed to massive displacement. In one case, within the first month following a 2014 US-led operation, close to one million Pashtuns became internally displaced persons (IDPs).

Second, Pashtuns were targeted by the foreign fighters (mostly Taliban members) fleeing Afghanistan. Once these foreign fighters settled in, they began to radicalize local youth—mostly unemployed graduates from Islamic seminaries—encouraging them to fight for Taliban rule in the region and for the return of the Taliban to Afghanistan. They also recruited youth to engage in extorting local businesses and in executing tribal vendettas (Gunaratna and Nielsen 2008). When tribal elders resisted the oppression of their people, at times through

---

[2] Mainly North Waziristan and South Waziristan, which both border Afghanistan. See Text Box 1 for an explanation of FATA and PATA, the tribal areas of Pakistan.

[3] The seven operations were: Operation Enduring Freedom (2001–2002); Operation Al Mizan (2002–2006), Operation Zalzala (2008); Operations Sher Dil in tribal district Bajaur (2008–2009), Rah-e-Haq in district Swat (2007), and Rah-e-Rast in district Swat (2009); Operation Rah-e-Nijat (2009–2010); Operation Zarb-e-Azab (2014); and Operation Radd-ul-Fassad (2017). Several minor operations were also launched, such as the Khyber-4 Operation in July 2017 which focused on the border areas inside the Khyber Agency—one of the seven agencies, or regions, of the erstwhile FATA.

> **Text Box 1: What Are the Tribal Areas?**
>
> The Federally Administered Tribal Areas (FATA) consisted of seven tribal regions (or agencies) in northwestern Pakistan. The seven regions, now called districts, are Bajaur, Khyber, Kurram, Mohmand, Orakzai, North Waziristan, and South Waziristan. Since the independence of Pakistan in 1947, the president of Pakistan has had absolute legislative and executive authority over the FATA. The Pakistan Constitution blocked parliament and constitutional courts from exercising any jurisdiction over the territory.
>
> The Provincially Administered Tribal Areas (PATA) include the northwestern Malakand division of the Khyber Pakhtunkhwa (KP) province. The governor of the KP province, a presidential appointee, has absolute authority in legislative and judicial matters of the PATA. The elected local members in the provincial legislative assembly of the KP do not have the power to initiate legislation concerning their districts. The Frontier Crimes Regulation (see **Text Box 2**), in contrast to the FATA, did not extend its jurisdiction over the PATA.
>
> In May 2018, following the rise of the Pashtun Tahafuz Movement, the FATA was given constitutional status under the 25th amendment of the Pakistan Constitution through its integration with the KP province. This amendment also abolished the status of the erstwhile PATA by empowering the elected members to initiate legislation concerning their local districts.

violent retaliation, the Taliban began assassinating them and attacking their families.[4] Meanwhile, the army and state intelligence have supported the Talibanization of the tribal region to discourage the creation of a Pashtun state that would encompass Afghanistan and Pakistan's northwestern Pashtun-majority areas.

Third, tribal Pashtuns have been victims of Pakistan's policies targeting the Taliban. In order to drive out the "Bad Taliban" (the TTP) from the region, Pakistan security forces formed local militias comprised of defectors from the TTP and local co-opted youth. Instead of stabilizing the region, these militias practice extortion of traders and shopkeepers and killing those who do not comply.[5] These militias have been integrated into the tribal community,

---

[4] In an interview with the author, Interviewee 6, a PTM coordinator in Islamabad, stated: "The voice of the PTM was raised by our *masharans* (local elders who hold traditional authority in Pashtun society) but their voice was suppressed. ... masharans who were local politicians and knew well about their local conflict dynamics were assassinated by 'na maloom afrad' (unknown assailants)."

[5] In an interview with the author, Interviewee 1, a male activist and PTM leader from district Tank, commented on the security establishment: "They are creating different groups of maliks, Talibans, and masharans in tribal areas.... They do not want to end their policy of supporting Talibans.... We do not accept Pashtuns getting killed."

joining government-backed Peace Committees charged with maintaining law and order. However, far from establishing peace, these groups have often been propagators of violence, attacking barber shops, music stores, and girls' schools for being anti-Islam in their eyes (Roggio 2008). Furthermore, the integration of Taliban defectors into local communities has exacerbated the tendency in Pakistan to racially profile Pashtuns as terrorists.

Pashtun youth recognized that they could not challenge state violence while using the same violent tools against their oppressors.

Finally, Pashtuns have suffered under punitive measures enacted by a Pakistani security policy that often conflates ethnicity with extremist ideology. When IDPs have returned to the region following government allowances, they have faced new challenges and constraints, including harassment at security checkpoints, land mines, extortion, enforced disappearances of local men, and targeted killings of tribal elders (Mehsud 2016).[6] The tribal Pashtuns had also been subject to a British Raj-era law, the Frontier Crimes Regulation (FCR), which until May 2018 deprived them of the right to seek justice and allowed the state to administer collective punishment against them in the form of property demolition and the enforced displacement of entire tribes (see Text Box 2 for more information on the FCR) ("Frontier Crimes Regulation" 2019).

Faced with this injustice, Pashtuns have largely chosen to express their grievances against the state in distinctly nonviolent ways, despite having opportunities to engage in violence. The arms bazaars of the tribal areas, which grew through support from the state and the West during the Cold War, have been identified as South Asia's biggest market of arms and ammunition. This burgeoning arms trade and weapon manufacturing industry has increased the presence and use of guns in communal disputes. Meanwhile, terrorist groups have been actively targeting Pashtun youth for recruitment. Yet Pashtun youth recognized that they could not challenge state violence while using the same violent tools against their oppressors. In the power vacuum that resulted from the assassinations of tribal elders, university-educated youth stepped up as leaders advocating for a return to a Pashtun tradition of nonviolent direct action that had first arisen in the 1920s and 1930s under the British Raj.

---

6   Local civilians and human rights organizations uncovered extrajudicial killings committed by both Pakistan security forces and militants. In August 2009, the Human Rights Commission of Pakistan discovered mass graves and reported the extrajudicial killing of suspected militants, their relatives, and suspected supporters. Human Rights Watch also reported extrajudicial killings of civilians.

Text Box 2: What is the FCR?*

In 1901, the British Raj in India passed the Frontier Crimes Regulation, a special law which instituted the practice of collective punishment to the present-day region of Pakistan, including Khyber Pakhtunkhwa, Balochistan and the FATA. Under this law, a tribal *jirga* (council) consisting of local *maliks* (government-appointed tribal leaders) could conduct the trial of a suspect and present its decision to the political agent (civil administrator appointed by the governor of the KP province) of the region. The political agent then decided the final conviction or acquittal of the suspect and was not bound to follow the jirga's decision. The political agent's decision could not be challenged before the higher courts.

Collective punishment functioned as follows:

1. All members of a village or tribe are held responsible for a murder if a dead body is found in their village.

2. A fine is imposed on the entire tribe or family for the wrongdoing of a single person.

3. If the fine is not paid by relatives of the offender, then the property of the offender is sold to pay for the fine.

The FCR ended in the KP province in 1956 and in Balochistan in 1973. However, the FATA remained under the FCR until May 2018, forming one of the PTM's early grievances against the state. It was only after the FATA integrated with the KP province that the FCR was de facto ended.

---

* For more information on the FCR, see Yousaf 2019.

II. Emergence of the Nonviolent Movement and Its First Actions

In 2013, a group of internally displaced university students started a grassroots movement in South Waziristan calling for the right to life and property for the Mehsud, a Pashtun tribe. Led by human rights activist Manzoor Pashteen (see Figure 1), the Mehsud Tahafuz Movement (MTM) demanded the demining of the Mehsud territory, impartial investigations and trials of those involved in the enforced disappearances of the tribe's men, the ending of humiliating practices against locals at security checkpoints, extortions, and targeted killings (whether by the Taliban or during military operations), and the provision of fair compensation for properties damaged as a result of the conflict ("Pashtun Tahafuz Movement" 2021). The voice of the MTM was absent from the media but the movement was gaining popularity among the local people of South Waziristan, North Waziristan, and Dera Ismail Khan—a northwestern city of the KP province that served as a convenient meeting place for supporters from adjacent tribal neighborhoods (see Map 1 on page 19).

In early January 2018, an IDP named Naqeebullah Mehsud was killed by police in Karachi on suspicion of ties to the Taliban. The MTM used the steady media coverage of this incident to draw attention to the violation of their rights. Seeking justice for Mehsud, the activists organized a long march from Dera Ismail Khan to Islamabad, covering a distance of more than 300 miles and passing through several cities of the KP and Punjab provinces. As the protestors drove their caravan of buses, wagons, cars, and motorcycles from city to city, Pashtuns from adjacent districts joined in support. By the time they reached Peshawar, the capital of the KP province, on the third day, they had decided that the MTM would be renamed the Pashtun Tahafuz Movement as they were seeking protection (*tahafuz*) for all Pashtuns, not only those of the Mehsud tribe. All of the Pashtun community had been subject to the same repressive policies, causing the same grievances. The movement now forged a unifying space for all ethnic Pashtuns.

After the marchers arrived in Islamabad, the Pakistani capital, they organized the All Pashtun Community Jirga in the form of a sit-in that began on February 1, 2018.[7] On the sixth day of the sit-in, a delegation of tribal elders that included PTM leader Pashteen met with the

> **Pashtun Voices:**
>
> "As Naqeebullah was a Mehsud and the MTM was created to protect the rights of Mehsud in the whole country, Naqeebullah's killing was one of the main triggers for raising support for the MTM. The MTM now got media attention that had been limited because there was no media access in SW from 2001 to 2015."
>
> —Interviewee 6, PTM Coordinator in Islamabad

---

7   A *jirga* is a Pashtun council in which tribal elders help to resolve local issues in consultation with maliks.

FIGURE 1: A Demonstration by the Mehsud Tahafuz Movement

In 2013, the youth of South Waziristan formed the Mehsud Tahafuz Movement. The Urdu sign reads: "The security institutions must be prevented from supporting the militancy." Manzoor Pashteen is pictured holding the English sign.

Pakistani prime minister and military leaders to raise the jirga's concerns. The delegation returned to the sit-in with a written agreement from the prime minister stating that senior policeman Rao Anwar had been suspended from government service due to his alleged role in the murder of Naqeebullah Mehsud, and that all resources would be deployed to bring him to justice through fair trial in court. The agreement also addressed other concerns of the PTM, including clearing land mines, financially compensating landmine victims, and establishing an intermediate college in Mehsud's name.

The *masharans* (local elders who hold traditional authority in Pashtun society), *maliks*,[8] and youth were divided in their response. The elders wanted to stop the sit-in immediately, while the maliks wanted to end the protest quietly in the middle of the night in order to appease the military. The youth pushed for a televised statement from the prime minister announcing his public commitment to address the Pashtuns' grievances, and wanted the establishment of a truth and reconciliation commission to hold accountable the military, maliks, and other government officials. Unable to agree with the protesting youth groups, the maliks took their buses and vans and left.

---

8   *Maliks* are local elites deputed by the state who are tasked with officiating these councils. The Maliki system was instituted by the British Raj in 1890 and the role is hereditary through a malik's son. Regarding maliks, PTM coordinator Interviewee 6 states, "Those people who are the upholders of British policy in Pashtun area are part of the government. They oppose the PTM. One of the biggest challenges we face from the local people is from system-supported maliks."

The youth leaders of the PTM continued the sit-in until they received further assurances from the government that the terms of the agreement would be met. They gave the government 30 days to fulfill its promise and warned that the sit-in would resume if their demands were not met. The government released 100 missing persons in a single day to slow the movement's momentum by appeasing the family members, relatives of missing persons, and civil society members (Khan 2018). Meanwhile, the PTM has continued its use of civil resistance strategies and tactics to achieve its six primary goals:

FIGURE 2: The Newly-Formed PTM Holds a Jalsa in Peshawar

1. Establishing a truth and reconciliation commission to investigate the human rights abuses committed during military operations in the Pashtun region;

2. Ending enforced disappearances;

3. Securing justice for the victims of enforced disappearances by ensuring free and fair trials for them in the courts;

4. Demining the tribal areas and removing the curfew in South Waziristan;

5. Ending extra-judicial killings; and

6. Stopping the humiliation of Pashtun families at security checkpoints.

> Pashtun Voices:
>
> "We demand the formation of a truth and reconciliation commission to expose wrongdoings of the military in the Pashtun region, but the military and the maliks do not agree on this. We want that this truth (the suppression of Pashtuns) should come before all Pashtuns. Is that why they have killed Pashtuns? Why they have humiliated us? So, we need a truth and reconciliation commission along with some international mediator, but the military does not agree. They still support the terrorists (e.g., Talibans and Peace Committees) in the Pashtun region.... We will not remain silent."
>
> —Interviewee 1, PTM leader from district Tank

III. Pragmatic Necessity for Nonviolent Resistance

The PTM's choice to use nonviolent resistance against the state was one of pragmatic necessity. Youth activists understood that the collective punishment measures afforded to the state under the Frontier Crimes Regulation made the use of armed resistance ineffective, futile, and self-destructive (see Text Box 2). The PTM leaders and activists learned about the consequences of using violence to demand rights from the Baloch movement. In an interview with the author, Interviewee 2, a male university student and PTM activist from Peshawar city, comments:

> *The Baloch resistance is violent, and the state has suppressed them in such a way that no one knows about their issues.... Our security institutions have been given training to suppress violence, so they can deal with violent resistance, but they cannot deal with nonviolent resistance.*[9]

Since 1947, ethnic Baloch resistance groups in Pakistan, such as the Baloch Liberation Army, have been waging a violent insurgency in the Balochistan province to fight for greater autonomy and control over their region's resources.[10] The government of Pakistan has launched various military operations against the Balochi nationalists. This has shaped the public perception in Pakistan and internationally that the Baloch are an equal participant in violent conflict rather than victims of oppression and injustice—a damage to their legitimate struggle for rights.[11] This lesson was not lost on the PTM, as one of their leaders from Peshawar city noted, "If we resort to violence, our political movement will be weakened and broken, such as was done with the Baloch resistance."[12]

In a speech at a *jalsa* (gathering) in Dera Ismail Khan on July 15, 2018, Manzoor Pashteen, founding leader of the PTM, shared that the source of the PTM's power is distinct from the army and militants who rely on guns. Pashteen emphasized:

> *We rely on the strength of our patience... the strength of our bravery... the strength of our love for our land... the strength of our bonds of respect and honor ("nang," see Text Box 3) with our mothers and sisters. We struggle against them (military and terrorists) with empty hands of nonviolence.*[13]

---

9 Interview with Interviewee 2, August 29, 2018.

10 Such as natural gas, copper, and gold.

11 Though there have been times when the insurgency has paused, such as in April 2016 when four commanders and 144 Balochistan Liberation Army fighters gave up armed resistance when reconciliation was offered by the state, the continuous human rights violations by security forces against the Baloch have pushed Baloch youth to continue in armed struggle against the state.

12 Interview with Interviewee 2, August 29, 2018.

13 THE CLICK PLUS [YouTube User], "Manzoor Pashteen Speech in DI Khan Jalsa," 2018.

IV. Historical Lessons for the PTM: Bacha Khan, His Red Shirt Movement, and the Cultural Norm of Nonviolent *Badal*

In guiding the movement in the use of nonviolent strategies, the leaders of the PTM have appealed to the legacy of Abdul Ghaffar Khan (known as *Bacha Khan,* or "King Khan"). Bacha Khan led the *Khudai Khidmatgars* ("Servants of God") in the Red Shirt Movement (RSM), a nonviolent resistance movement against the British Raj in what is now Pakistan that at its peak in the 1930s was comprised of over 100,000 Pashtuns. Bacha Khan educated Pashtun youth in debate, dialogue, and reasoning skills, and worked to reform Pashtun tribal norms into a nonviolent philosophy that would guide the movement (Khan 1997). His teachings and strategies have exerted significant influence on the PTM's practice of nonviolent resistance (see Table 1).

A male PTM activist from Islamabad shared that this influence is due in part to the similar grievances between the current conflict in the Pashtun region and the oppression this region experienced under the yoke of the British military. He comments:

> *The nature of Pakistan's government policy in the Pashtun region is similar to the British colonial policy (e.g., the Maliki system and the Frontier Crimes Regulation). Bacha Khan and Khan Shaheed[14] resisted the colonial policy with nonviolent actions. The entire leadership of the PTM is inspired by the ideology of Bacha Khan and Khan Shaheed. Therefore, the PTM has renewed the strategies of Bacha Khan.[15]*

In order to successfully promote nonviolent resistance, Bacha Khan sought to reform an important aspect of the *Pashtunwali*. The *Pashtunwali*, or "way of the Pashtuns," is the code that traditional Pashtuns live by. In this way of life, justice functions through *badal* (reciprocation), which necessitates that a person defends their honor—with violence, if needed (see Text Box 3 on page 13).

---

14 Abdul Samad Khan Achakzai (1907–1973), also known as "Khan Shaheed" or "Balochi Gandhi," was a Pashtun nationalist and social reformer from the present-day province of Balochistan in Pakistan. Inspired by Bacha Khan and Gandhi, he committed himself to nonviolent resistance to secure freedom from British rule. In 1930, at the age of 23, he led a civil disobedience movement in Balochistan against the British Raj (Source: *The Pashtun Times*).

15 Interview with Interviewee 6, August 10, 2018.

Table 1: A Comparison of the RSM and the PTM

THE RED SHIRT MOVEMENT (RSM) 1930s	THE PASHTUN TAHAFUZ MOVEMENT (PTM) 2018 – PRESENT
The RSM emerged in response to the British troops' violent repression of Pashtuns.	The PTM emerged in response to the violent repression of Pashtuns by terrorist organizations and Pakistan's security forces.
The nonviolent methods of the RSM included marches, processions, hunger strikes, boycotts of British goods, picketing to prevent people from entering government buildings, and spontaneous strikes.	The nonviolent methods of the PTM include long marches, processions in bazaars and markets, reactionary protests (such as in response to the arrest of activists), and jalsas.
The symbolic clothing of the RSM was originally a white dress, which later changed to the Red Shirt.	The symbolic clothing of the PTM is a mosaic-patterned (red, black, and white) Pashteen hat.
The RSM commemorated the incidents of atrocity committed against its supporters.	The PTM commemorates killings and enforced disappearances of its activists, via social media memes and processions.
The RSM started a magazine, the "Pakhtun," to spread its message of nonviolence in Pashtun society.	The PTM organizes study circles designed to promote messages of nonviolence and nonviolent actions among educated youth.
The RSM established village jirgas to resolve local disputes through dialogue instead of violent badal.	The PTM approaches constitutional courts for remedy in cases of forcefully disappeared persons, killings, and arrests.
The RSM engaged in nonviolent interventions, such as holding marches in public places, even when British troops directly fired at them. For example, on August 24, 1931, the RSM organized a protest at the Hathikhel village, in the district of Banu of the KP province, despite British restrictions; more than 80 RSM activists were killed by British troops' gunfire.	The PTM wages nonviolent interventions, such as holding marches and processions through army checkpoints, even though activists are killed and injured by soldiers. For example, on May 26, 2019, 14 PTM activists were killed and around 40 were injured in a firing at the Kharqamar checkpoint in North Waziristan.
The RSM worked on equal rights for women, resisted the *purdah* ("full-face veil") and was successful in mobilizing women to participate in public life.	The PTM engages women at various levels of the movement. Women are leaders, activists, and supporters of the PTM.

Badal is adjudicated in tribal jirgas where both the victim and the perpetrator present their cases to a council of elders who determine an appropriate settlement. Victims have retaliated with violence when unsatisfied with a jirga's results or when the perpetrator fails to abide by the ruling. Under the British Raj, Pashtun clergy used badal to mobilize armed resistance.[16] In response, Bacha Khan worked to transform badal into a mechanism for seeking justice through nonviolent means.

Bacha Khan encouraged his followers to give up tribal feuding which had often led to a cycle of violent badal. He emphasized the importance of Pashtun freedom fighters avoiding violent jihad against colonial injustice, as they would be labeled as rebels and their struggle would lose legitimacy. He instead stressed the merits of forbearance, forgiveness, and self-restraint while using tactics such as marches, strikes, and boycotts to resist oppression (Banerjee 2000).

---

16   Among them was Ghazi Mirzali Khan (1897–1960), commonly known as "the Faqir of Ipi," who was a Pashtun tribal religious leader from North Waziristan. He mobilized a tribal militia to wage jihad against British colonial rule. In 1936, he led a campaign against the British troops at Khaisor town of the Bannu district, in which a large number of casualties and destruction occurred.

FIGURE 3: A PTM Supporter, Along with His Children, Holds a Frame Containing Photos of Bacha Khan and PTM Leader Manzoor Pashteen.

Following in Bacha Khan's footsteps, the PTM calls for nonviolent badal instead of the violent badal that has become intertwined with extremist notions of jihad. The PTM members have stressed the use of nonviolent tactics alongside the traditional process of badal in order to secure justice. In appealing to the international community for support, they have drawn parallels between badal and constitutional justice. They call for a truth and reconciliation commission to function as a type of international jirga in which the perpetrators (i.e., the Taliban, the army, and the government) sit with representatives of the victims (i.e., the PTM leaders and tribal elders), facilitated by the United Nations Office in Geneva.

Pashtun Voices:

"We have the philosophy of nonviolence of Bacha Khan which teaches us to remain non-violent while seeking justice."

— Interviewee 4, PTM's European regional coordinator in Denmark

Text Box 3: What is the *Pashtunwali* Code?*

Pashtunwali, "the way of the Pashtuns," is the conventional code of life for traditional Pashtuns living in Pakistan and Afghanistan. The main principles of *Pashtunwali* pertinent to this study are *nanawatey, nang,* and *badal*.

Nanawatey, "asylum" or "protection," is giving shelter to anyone who requests shelter from their enemies. The host is obligated to honor the request, even if it comes from a former enemy. The host who gives *nanawatey* defends the asylum seeker, even at the cost of his own life. It is under this code that, in 2001, some local Pashtuns in the tribal areas gave asylum to the foreign fighters who had requested refuge from the Americans and their allied forces in Afghanistan.

Nang, "honor," is the commitment of any Pashtun—who regards his honor to be more sacred than his life—to defend the weak. For instance, the foreign militants portrayed themselves as weak when they requested *nanawatey* from local elders.

Badal, "reciprocation," is the right to keep *nang* intact and is necessary for remediating dishonor, whether a minor taunt or a murder. Bacha Khan strove to reform *badal* into nonviolent means in Pashtun society. For example, Khan established the village jirga to resolve disputes through dialogue and forgiveness instead of violent revenge. The PTM seeks justice to regain the lost pride or honor of Pashtuns using nonviolent methods instead of violent means.

---

*   Information drawn from Banting 2003.

V. PTM Leadership: Diversity of Membership and Women's Participation

Though the PTM draws inspiration and strategies from Bacha Khan's Red Shirt Movement, a noteworthy difference is that the PTM is led by youth instead of elders and by a collective rather than a single charismatic leader. Manzoor Pashteen, though a well-spoken and prominent figurehead, is not the sole leader of the movement, nor do the day-to-day operations of the organization depend on his leadership—evidenced by the continued campaigning of the PTM when he has been incarcerated. The youth leaders and frontline activists of the PTM are predominantly lawyers,[17] political and human rights activists, university graduates, and other members of the Pashtun intelligentsia, which has contributed to an internal culture that respects tribal norms while advancing Pashtun rights in accordance with international standards.

The PTM initially organized its leadership into the Central Core Committee, a temporary transitional body whose role was to develop a constitution for the group. The committee had diverse representation, including members of religious and ethnic minorities. However, it was dismantled in the last week of April 2019 after a draft constitution could not be finalized. Efforts to reorganize were cut short the following month due to the arrests of a large number of prominent leaders.

Outside the central leadership, the PTM has a network of coordinators at various levels across Pakistan and abroad. This network mobilizes support at the district and international levels. At the district level, local activists and provincial coordinators work together to run campaign events. This partnership allows for the movement to maintain a coherent focus across regions while tailoring each event to the particulars of a campaign's location. At the international level, the diaspora community works to raise international support for Pashtun rights. For example, the Pashtun community in Canada has created the Pashtun Global Diaspora to organize and mobilize 2 million diasporic Pashtuns to raise their voices for peace and rights in the Pashtun regions in Pakistan and Afghanistan (Pashtun Global Diaspora 2019).

> **Pashtun Voices:**
>
> "Every young person of 20 to 30 years of age is part of this movement because they have grown up during this war. You see in the PTM mostly the educated class, especially university students, who are leaders."
>
> — Interviewee 4, PTM coordinator in Denmark

---

17   Including Ali Wazir and Mohsin Dawar.

FIGURE 4: Tweet by PTM Activist Tariq

In this October 3, 2018, tweet, PTM activist Tariq shares a photo of a gathering led by Bacha Khan during Mohandas Gandhi's visit to the current KP province (ex-North-West Frontier Province, NWFP). By circling in red the women in the photo, Tariq is emphasizing the inclusive nature of both the Red Shirt Movement and the Pashtun Protection Movement while venting his anger over the Talibanization of Pashtun society during the Afghan–Soviet War in the 1980s that reversed Bacha Khan's reforms.

The inclusivity of leadership has been mirrored in the diversity of membership in the PTM as a strategy for success. The movement is inclusive of activists from various demographics and political parties. These include civil society members (e.g., Pakistan's human rights, women's rights, and religious minority rights activists), the left-wing political parties of Pakistan (excluding the pro-government Pashtun political elite), and victims of violence. According to Interviewee 3, one of the PTM's woman leaders in Islamabad, the movement is a loosely structured spectrum of ethno-nationalists, feminists, leftists, and those affected by terrorism and violence. Another one of the PTM's woman leaders and a member of the PTM's Central

FIGURE 5: Tweet by PTM Leader Sanna Ejaz.

In this tweet, Sanna Ejaz challenges the threats to her life from intelligence agencies, especially ISI, by reiterating her commitment to the protection of human rights through nonviolent resistance, as Bacha Khan did.

Core Committee comments, "We try to reach out to all people. We believe if oppression happened to us, it must not happen to anyone else."[18]

Women of all ages are breaking through cultural impediments of participation in public life as leaders, activists, and supporters of the movement. Women have organized, mobilized, and arranged logistics for campaigns, they have educated and pursued education, and they have entered political life and used their positions as activists and politicians to increase the reach of the movement's messaging. Women have also managed the stage during protests, led protests, and have contributed to publications. Women leaders are also establishing libraries in the Pashtun region to spread education among women (Kazam 2021; Ejaz 2021). One woman leader explains that "In our region, women never used to come out from the rural areas to participate in such movements. For the first time our units [of the Women Democratic Front] came out from the rural areas and we connected them with the PTM."[19]

According to Interviewee 6, women supporters of the PTM are comprised of students, rights activists, political leaders, and victims of war, whose social and economic status has

---

18   Interview with Interviewee 5, September 10, 2018.

19   Interview with Interviewee 3, August 26, 2018.

been negatively affected by the killings, enforced disappearances, and permanent physical injuries of their male family members. He explains:

> *The oppression and atrocities have not made a distinction between a male and a female. In cases of an abduction or extrajudicial killing of a male member of a family, male and female are both affected. Therefore, both men and women have come out [to participate in the PTM actions].*[20]

Women activists of the PTM have faced harsh crackdown measures by the state authorities, including being named in malicious police cases, placed on Exit Control Lists (no-fly lists), illegally detained, having their family homes raided, and receiving death threats (see Figure 5). In one case, PTM activist Gulalai Ismail was forced to escape the country after being placed on a state kill list.

A diverse membership, including women's involvement, has had a tangible influence on the PTM's public outreach to other movements. The PTM has, for example, expressed solidarity with women's movements of other ethnic minorities of Pakistan. Baloch and Sindhi women have been leading nonviolent campaigns to secure information about missing persons and the release of political prisoners in the Balochistan and Sindh provinces. On November 12, 2018, at a women-led Voice for Baloch Missing Persons protest in Quetta, Balochistan, one of the PTM leaders, Mullah Behram, gave a speech in solidarity with the women's movement. Likewise, on December 5, 2020, Manzoor Pashteen met with ethnic Sindhi activists in Sindh province who have been protesting and demanding the recovery of Sindhi missing persons (Pashteen 2020). PTM leadership is also famous among Hindu youth, a religious minority within the country (Bukhari 2020).

---

20   Interview with Interviewee 6, August 10, 2018.

VI. Movement Strategies and Tactics

Disruptive Tactics

Since its emergence in 2018, the PTM has employed nonviolent tactics such as jalsas, sit-ins, long marches, processions, and demonstrations in large Pakistani cities to advance Pashtun rights. *Jalsas*, a prominent PTM tactic, are large gatherings followed by speeches with crowds that can number in the low thousands to over 50,000 people. The first wave of jalsas began at the movement's inaugural February 2018 sit-in in Islamabad and lasted through May of the same year, when the tribal areas were given constitutional status as a result of the integration of the FATA into the KP province. After a series of unsuccessful dialogues with the government, the PTM resumed holding jalsas. A second wave of jalsas occurred from January 2019 until April of that year—ending when the government arrested several PTM leaders and charged them with sedition. A third wave of jalsas have been organized in 2020, following the arrest of Manzoor Pashteen and continue, with the Jalsa in Peshawar City held on February 7, 2021, where the PTM criticized foreign governments' financial support for the Pakistani government and military (see Map 1).

Whenever the PTM wants to hold a campaign event such as a jalsa, the local district committee is responsible for making all arrangements. They begin by establishing district-level campaign teams responsible for managing logistics, applying for the No Objection Certificate (NOC) permit required by the state to hold a rally, and mobilizing the local community. The members of the central leadership visit the event location a week before the event to mobilize support. For example, leaders Manzoor Pashteen, Mohsin Dawar, Ali Wazir, and other activists visited the towns, villages, and cities of the erstwhile FATA and the KP, along with other Pakistani cities (such as Islamabad and Rawalpindi) to increase participation in the Pashtun Long March to Bannu (referred to as #PashtunLongMarch2Bannu on social media), held on January 2, 2020, at Mandan Park in Bannu.

Communication Strategies

Activists use their mobile phones to join closed groups on social media in which PTM central leadership and district-level coordinators collaborate, plan, and determine strategy. In an interview with the author, an activist in Denmark who coordinates the PTM's activities across

> **Pashtun Voices:**
> "Our activists from other cities go to that city about one week before the jalsa, meet with the local committees and run campaigns in the area to communicate message to the people."
> — Interviewee 6, PTM coordinator in Islamabad

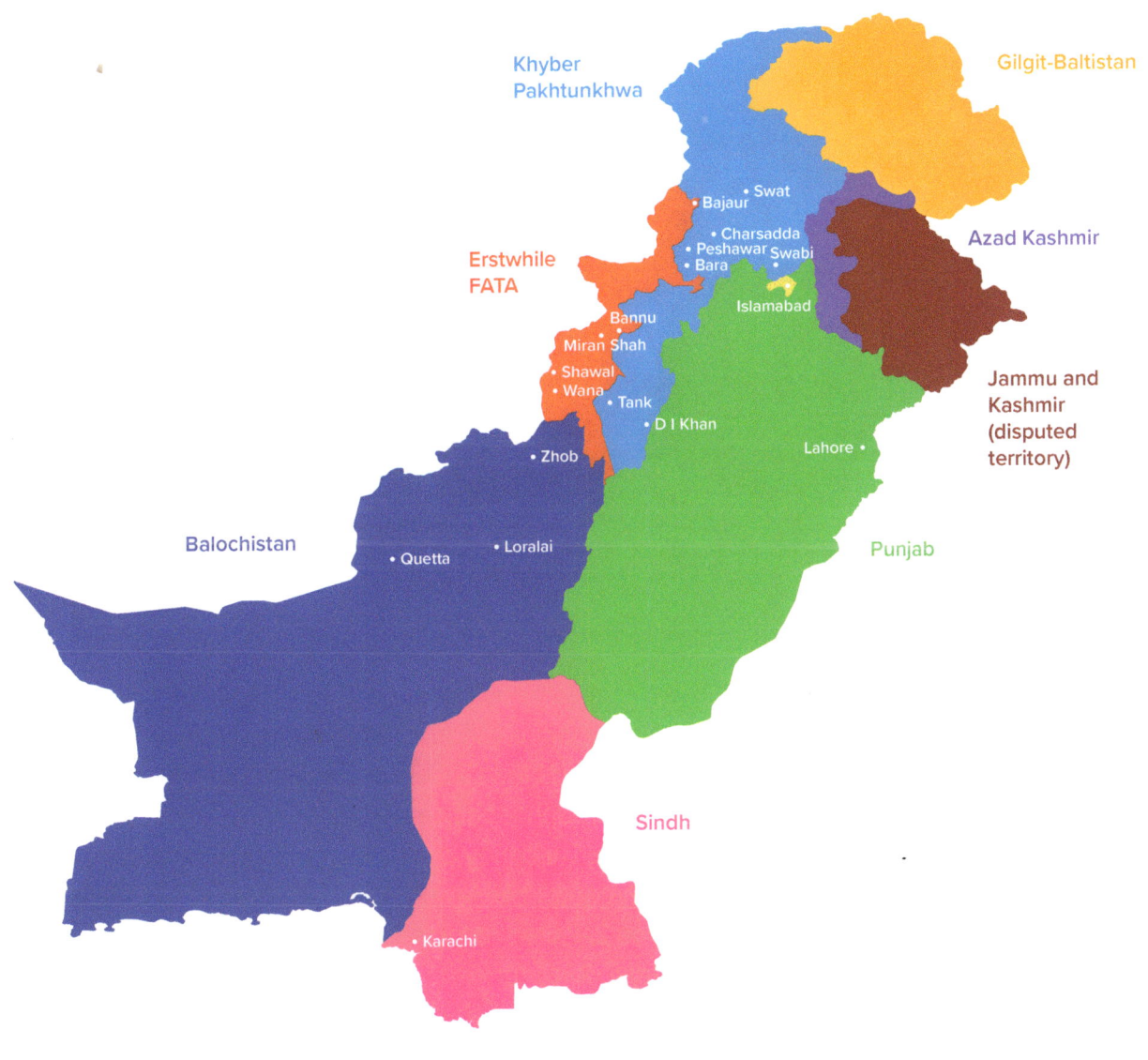

Map 1. Locations of PTM Jalsas in 2018–2020

Jalsas in 2018: Peshawar (January 28 and April 8); Islamabad (following the sit-in on February 1-10); Bajaur (February 20); Zhob (March 10); Quetta (March 11); Bara (March 18); Wana (April 14); Mochi Gate in Lahore (April 22); Swat (April 29); Karachi (May 13); Dera Ismail Khan (July 15); Swabi (August 12); and Bannu (October 28).
Jalsas in 2019: Tank (January 13); Wana (March 15); Peshawar (March 31); Miran Shah (April 14).
Jalsas in 2020: Bannu (January 12); Loralai (February 9); Dera Ismail Khan (Feb 16); Charsadda (March 1); Shawal (August 8); Wana (September 20); Miran Shah (November 15); Karachi (December 6); and Bara (December 27).

Europe offers some information on the group's use of social media. "We have special teams on social media. They work to make contacts with all the stakeholders. These teams work on Facebook, WhatsApp, Skype, Twitter and Viber.... We send them messages via phone calls and Facebook to contact activists."[21]

---

21   Interview with Interviewee 6, July 31, 2018.

FIGURE 6: Manzoor Pashteen Addresses a Gathering to Promote Participation in the Long March to Bannu

The PTM uses these social media resources to publicly disseminate movement messages. Leaders use Twitter to initiate messaging campaigns, and activists livestream speeches, jalsa proceedings, and press conferences on Facebook. News media outlets pick up PTM stories from social media and extend the activists' reach through legacy media such as print and television. The "international media take stories from there. Then they contact us, conduct interviews with us and make videos and documentaries,"[22] comments Interviewee 3. For example, in April 2018, the French state-owned television station, France 24, aired a documentary on the emergence, grievances, and nonviolent actions of the PTM featuring interviews with PTM members.

In order to reach supporters who do not have internet access or aptitude, PTM activists also communicate through pamphlets, banners, handbills, graffiti, loudspeakers mounted on minivans, and door-to-door campaigns. Woman educator and PTM leader from District Swat, Interviewee 5, describes the movement's approach as follows:

First, we hire a small vehicle, fix a loudspeaker on it and make announcements in different areas. Our elders speak on the loudspeakers. Second, we distribute pamphlets. Third, we do a door-to-door campaign.[23]

This alternative approach is particularly important to circumvent the government's frequent suspension of mobile and internet services in the tribal areas. Interviewee 3 shares,

---

22   Interview with Interviewee 3, August 26, 2018.

23   Interview with Interviewee 5, September 10, 2018.

"In SW when the military disconnects the landlines, we use small posters and flyers."[24] Prior to hosting jalsas, flyers about the event are distributed at homes and public places such as universities, hospitals, markets, government offices, and transport terminals (see Figure 7).

Constructive Organizing and Creative Actions

PTM activists are creating parallel grassroots institutions to promote nonviolent solutions and, more specifically, prevent violent jihadis from recruiting and radicalizing Pashtun youth. Activists have established study centers and host study circles in which youth are provided an opportunity to engage with philosophy of nonviolent actions through book readings, discussions, poems, and songs. For example, Interviewee 5 founded Ghandara Centre for Peace and Culture Education where she works to promote values such as justice and equality in Pashtun society through different activities like creating art, poetry, and music (Ghandara 2020). She comments:

FIGURE 7: A PTM Activist Carries a Bundle of Flyers to Distribute Among the Local Public.

> *We are countering violence on multiple levels. We are trying to open study circles at various places. In those centers we will read books and hold discussions about nonviolent movements. PTM youth write songs and poems on peace and we intend to promote them.*[25]

In Peshawar city, the PTM has created the Friday Circles initiative, where they invite prominent Pashtun writers, historians, intellectuals, and activists to share their ideas with young participants of the Circles. These discussions include topics such as women rights, civic participation, democracy, the constitution of Pakistan, and Pashtun history, including the anti-Raj struggles of Bacha Khan and Khan Shaheed and the rise of religious extremism in Pashtun society since the Afghan–Soviet War in the 1980s. As part of these circles, PTM

---

24 Interview with Interviewee 3, August 26, 2018.

25 Interview with Interviewee 5, September 10, 2018.

FIGURE 8: Tweet by PTM Leader Mohsin Dawar.

leaders and activists organize talks and conferences on the strategies of nonviolent organizing and actions to counter violent extremism in the Pashtun region.

PTM musicians have also deployed their talents to counter the state's propaganda that portrays Pashtuns as innately violent. The Pakistani band Khumariyaan draws on Pashtun folk music and uses an ancient Pashtun instrument called a *rubab* to create music that honors Pashtun culture. Band member Sparlay Rawail—who is also a member of the PTM—remarks, "If the narrative is that Pashtuns are backward, they're not well educated, they don't know how to be 'civilized,' and they don't know how to create art and be creative, then certainly we are breakings stereotypes."[26]

An important part of the constructive organizing are the PTM's strategies for resource acquisition to be able to carry out and sustain its activities. The PTM finances its operations primarily through cash donations. Pashtun traders, businesspeople, professionals, and common people fund the movement's activities. Donations are collected at PTM events to help cover operation expenses. Interviewee 5 comments, "At jalsas we move small boxes among the public and people from all social classes, everyone—from professor to businessman—donates according to their capacity" (Khan 2021). Leaders also make their own financial contributions to cover petty expenses such as printing and photocopying of handbills, pamphlets, and banners.

In order for supporters to attend PTM events, the local PTM teams arrange transportation by collecting money from the attendees and coordinating the rental of buses and vans to bring the participants to jalsas and marches. Interviewee 5 notes, "All expenses people cover

---

26   Interview with Interviewee 3, August 26, 2018.

FIGURE 9: Activists Collect Funds at a PTM Jalsa.

themselves in order to participate in the jalsa. The jalsa participants arrange their transportation using their own resources."[27]

Beyond monetary resources, the movement is sustained through the labor of volunteers and professionals. PTM members have given thousands of volunteer hours to the movement through advertising work and attending events or by establishing and running parallel institutions to strengthen their communities. Professionals provide specialized labor to support the movement's cause, with lawyers arguing cases in court and politicians advocating in parliament. Thus, the PTM is supported through the voluntary contribution of funds and labor from a cross-section of Pashtun society.

Strategic Integration of Civil Resistance with Institutional Efforts

The PTM complements their use of civil resistance with taking action through established legal and political channels. Since many PTM leaders are lawyers and other professionals, they have the knowledge and skills necessary to engage in lawsuits, as noted by a woman activist from Islamabad: "We also go to legal battles, negotiations, and dialogue. We defend against attacks through resistance driven by legal activism and remaining resilient."[28]

---

27 Interview with Interviewee 5, September 10, 2018.

28 Interview with Interviewee 3, August 26, 2018.

FIGURE 10: Youth Sit on the Roof of a Bus to Travel to a PTM Jalsa.

Some PTM leaders have campaigned and won political positions, such as Mohsin Dawar and Ali Wazir, who both secured membership in the National Assembly, Pakistan's lower legislative house, as independents representing tribal area constituencies in the July 2018 elections. In addition to using these elected positions to influence government policy, they have leveraged their political positions to disseminate PTM messaging.

On October 1, 2019, in a historic speech on the floor of the National Assembly following his release from a pre-trial detention, Mohsin Dawar described the core PTM tenets, what it stood for, and emphasized its commitment to remaining nonviolent:

We are followers of nonviolence by faith. We're followers of Bacha Khan. We hate violence. PTM has emerged against violence. PTM has emerged against this war. Even if someone tries to push us towards violence we will not resort to violence. 14 of us have been killed [in the Kharkamar massacre]. Even if 1,400 are killed, even if 14,000 are killed, even if 140,000 are killed we will not resort to violence. This is our promise to our nation. But we will speak. We will tell the facts to the world.[29]

---

[29] Power TV Talk Shows [YouTube user], "Mohsin Dawar Speech in National Assembly Today," October 1, 2019.

VII. State Repression and PTM Strategies to Maintain Nonviolent Discipline

Repression and Propaganda Against the PTM

The state views the PTM as a national security threat in cahoots with hostile neighbors and that undermines Pakistani nationalism and the state by promoting a distinct Pashtun national identity. On May 28, 2019, in a speech on the floor of the National Assembly of Pakistan, SAFRON Minister Shehryar Afridi criticized the alleged anti-state actions of PTM leaders Mohsin Dawar and Ali Wazir and claimed that the movement's criticism of the security establishment benefits India and Afghanistan.[30] The army, meanwhile, claims that these countries' intelligence agencies fund the PTM (Syed and Raza 2019). The movement's refusal to use violence has left some members of Pakistan's security establishment frustrated that the PTM is "difficult to control," since they cannot crack down on the movement as they have done with the Baloch armed resistance (Masood, Mashal, and ur-Rehman 2019). However, this has not kept security forces from using violence against activists. Through the military and other proxies, the state has at times cracked down on the PTM with severe violence. One PTM leader even fled the country after learning her name was on a kill list. More commonly, prominent leaders have been arrested and charged with sedition.

One strategy of the state has been to use the Taliban defector-led Peace Committees as proxies for government violence. A Peace Committee in Wana, South Waziristan, banned the traditional Pashteen hats worn by the PTM on June 2, 2018. PTM leader Ali Wazir began planning a sit-in to protest the ban but the campaign was cut short when the Peace Committee asked him to leave town. When he refused, they attacked a market, drawing PTM supporters in protest. After the Peace Committee members left, the military arrived and continued the attack on civilians. Seven activists were killed and more than two dozen were injured. Support for the PTM only increased. In the following month, Wazir and Dawar were elected to the National Assembly.

The military has also directly instigated violent attacks on PTM activists, such as in the case of the Kharkamar massacre. On May 26, 2019, PTM activists were demonstrating at the Kharkamar security checkpoint to protest the military's beating of a local woman. The military shot into the crowd, killing 14 and wounding 25, and then arrested several of the remaining activists, including Wazir and Dawar.

---

30 SAFRON, or the Federal Ministry for States and Frontier Regions, is responsible for dealing with tribal areas. The tribal maliks work under the authority of SAFRON. Minister Afridi belongs to an influential Pashtun tribe that is closely intertwined with the Pakistani local, provincial, and federal governments.

FIGURE 11: Tweet by PTM Leader Manzoor Pashteen.

In addition to violence, another strategy of the state has been to manufacture a counter-movement to foster anti-PTM sentiment and discourage Pashtun mobilization. The Pakistan Protection Movement was created by the army and is comprised of Pashtuns who are former and current civil and military officers. The name—"Pakistan Protection Movement", a derivative of the PTM—aims to blur the distinction between and sow confusion about the "Pashtun Protection (Tahafuz) Movement" that uses the same acronym. The group has organized parallel rallies in the cities of Swat, Bajaur, and Swabi of Khyber Pakhtunkhwa. Leaders of these rallies delivered anti-PTM speeches that called PTM leaders and activists "foreign agents" (PTMO 2020).

The state has also used disinformation against the movement. They have tried to change the public's understanding of the Pashtun word *badal*, as used by the PTM, by replacing it with the Urdu cognate *badla*. The latter, which means "vengeance" or "revenge," has not been influenced by Bacha Khan's reforms and remains associated with violence. During a press conference on April 29, 2019, a Pakistani military spokesperson stated that the PTM leaders "say they want to take badla. What kind of badla [do] they want? Can they take badla on the army?" (ISPR Official 2019). They have thus tried to frame the movement as a violent threat to the state.

At the behest of the military, provincial governments have waged propaganda campaigns against the PTM activists. For example, in September 2018, the Punjab government released a state-funded public service announcement about suspected terrorists. This television advertisement was part of a larger campaign during the Islamic month of Muharram designed to prevent sectarian violence. However, the ad featured PTM leaders Manzoor Pashteen,

Mohsin Dawar, and Ali Wazir, and identified them as promoters of sectarian hate speech and violence. This attack backfired. As a result of public uproar—particularly on social media—the government pulled the images of the PTM leaders from the advertisement (Daily Times 2018).

PTM Nonviolent Discipline in the Face of Repression

PTM leaders work to build activists' resolve to remain nonviolent through reverence and deference to the teachings of iconic cultural heroes, particularly Bacha Khan. Most of the leaders and activists of the PTM are his loyal followers, calling themselves "Bacha Khanis." They frequently circulate his messages about the importance of nonviolent behavior in their public speeches, through interviews, and on social media. Speaking to this loyalty, Interviewee 3 notes, "The PTM character has no violence. Bacha Khanis are nonviolent."[31]

On the question of their commitment to nonviolent strategies, a PTM activist from Peshawar has argued that the PTM is fully aware of the consequences that would stem from the use of violence. Referencing Bacha Khan's teachings while under the British Raj, Interviewee 2 explains:

> *The PTM follows the philosophy of Bacha Khan who was a realist and believed in the existence of real constraining conditions. Real for him meant: if you pick up a gun, in two to three days you will be labeled a traitor and will be crushed violently. And no one will listen to your voice. No one will raise their voices in your support. Whereas in nonviolence, you fight, you remain in the field, you do not harm anyone and you get more support from neutral people.*[32]

In order to maintain nonviolent discipline following critical events of repression, PTM leaders redirect activists' energies toward backfire. They memorialize victims of oppression on social media, thus exposing the wrongdoing of the state while weakening the state's capacity to portray the victims as guilty of crime. The movement also leverages these social media campaigns into direct actions on the ground. One PTM coordinator explains, "In cases of arrests and ban on rallies, we run various posts and threads on social media, including Facebook and Twitter."[33] For example, following the police killing of PTM leader Arman Luni in Balochistan on March 31, 2019, they initiated the Facebook and Twitter hashtag #PeshawarLongMarch4Arman. The social media campaign culminated in a long march from South Waziristan to Peshawar, demanding the police register a First Information Report (the first document prepared by a

---

31 Interview with Interviewee 3, August 26, 2018.

32 Interview with Interviewee 2, August 29, 2018.

33 Interview with Interviewee 6, August 10, 2018.

police officer to initiate the criminal investigation of an offense) against the officer responsible for Luni's death and release other detained PTM activists.

Practical measures to maintain nonviolent discipline include avoiding direct confrontations with security forces, banning weapons at campaign events, and regularly reiterating their commitment to refraining from violence. As a PTM leader from Islamabad reveals, "No one can bring weapons in the marches and jalsas. Time and again, people are instructed to avoid violence."[34] On one occasion when Manzoor Pashteen was physically prevented by security forces from traveling to Karachi to address a jalsa, leadership took the opportunity to urge their supporters to remain nonviolent. As one activist shares:

> *In the midst of these oppressive policies all were instructed by the leadership that no one will resort to violence. Manzoor Pashteen maintains a stand since the very first day that we should remain nonviolent in all gatherings.*[35]

---

34 Interview with Interviewee 3, August 26, 2018.

35 Interview with Interviewee 4, July 31, 2018.

VIII. Impacts of the PTM

In an interview with the author, a woman leader from Swat notes that due to PTM work and pressure, "some of the missing persons are released, land mines in some areas are being cleared, the number of check posts are reduced, and the police is replacing the army at those check posts."[36]

Indeed, the PTM has had a significant impact on the tribal areas. The rise of the movement has fostered unity among the tribes by reducing tribal feuds through the facilitation of tribal jirgas and covenants. For example, on May 3, 2018, the PTM convened a jirga of elders from the Ahmadzai and Utmanzai, two influential tribes of South and North Waziristan, who pledged to remain united against rights violations and injustice experienced by tribal people. The jirga issued the statement: "We will remain united for the safety, rights violations, and injustice of our people. This resolution is neither against any state nor oppressive against any other state. If someone from Ahmadzai and Utmanzai tribes violates provisions of this jirga, he will be fined between 3 to 5 million rupees."[37]

On February 5, 2021, a Grand Peace Jirga was brokered by PTM leaders in Waziristan. The jirga issued a statement, signed by 120 member representatives from all tribes of the tribal areas, demanding that the military should hand over security and civil administrative matters to police and civilian authorities and leave the area. Moreover, the jirga demanded that 10,000 local youth should be employed in police and civil offices, which became possible due to the abolition of Frontier Crimes Regulation (FCR) in 2018 after the pressure from the PTM (Naya Dour 2021; Dawar 2021).

The PTM's nonviolent resistance has strengthened the protection of rights for the Pashtun people in Pakistan. In an alliance with the Tribal Women's Organization and the Tribal Youth Organization, the PTM had been demanding the abolition of the Frontier Crimes Regulation, the law which allowed the government and military to act in the tribal areas with impunity. In mid-2018, the government yielded to their campaign by introducing constitutional reforms in the FATA and integrating the tribal region into the KP province—an important demand of the PTM to ensure government accountability and curtail military abuses. Since the FCR only had jurisdiction over the FATA, the merger with the KP province effectively dissolved the FATA and thus the power of the FCR. The KP provincial government has since been establishing

---

36   Interview with Interviewee 5, September 10, 2018.

37   The source of this information is a video and photos of the jirga proceedings that were collected by the author during the research fieldwork on the Pashtun Tahafuz Movement.

constitutional institutions in the newly merged tribal districts, including a court system, a police service, and health, education, and welfare agencies.

The PTM is filling the leadership vacuum in the tribal areas by elevating youth and women into positions of political influence. Following the FATA–KP merger, which for the first time allowed the residents of the erstwhile FATA to have representation in Pakistan's National Assembly, Mohsin Dawar and Ali Wazir—two founding members of the PTM—won National Assembly seats as independent candidates in the Pakistani general elections held in May 2018. Their electoral victories were the product of the political stature they both gained as leaders of the PTM.

The rise of the PTM has fostered unity among the tribes by reducing tribal feuds through the facilitation of tribal jirgas and covenants.

By including women in the movement's leadership publicly and behind the scenes, the PTM has been breaking stereotypes that tribal women cannot participate in public life. Many women join the PTM jalsas, marches, and sit-ins as leaders, activists, and supporters, and these forums have offered them the opportunity to engage in discussions and decision-making on important social, economic, and political issues. The FATA–KP merger has also increased representation for women in the local government, which added 21 seats to the provincial assembly to account for the erstwhile FATA. Four of these seats are reserved for women, which has raised the number of female representatives to 26 out of 145 total in the assembly. Tribal women now have the power to make laws regarding key issues relevant to their communities.

The PTM had another major victory on January 29, 2019, when Prime Minister Imran Khan approved the recommended amendments to the Pakistan Penal Code that declared enforced disappearances a criminal offense. Over the subsequent year, targeted killings in the tribal areas declined by approximately 40 percent, according to the Center for Research & Security Studies Islamabad (CRSSI 2019).

PTM actions have also resulted in the removal of land mines, the easing of movement for local tribal Pashtuns through security checkpoints, and the return of many missing persons who had been victims of enforced disappearances. At an April 30, 2019, press conference, an army spokesperson[38] responding to PTM demands stated that "45 percent of the mined area had been cleared … [the] number of checkpoints decreased [and] the number of missing persons had also dropped to 2,500" (Bukhari 2020) from the original list of 8,000 persons that the PTM had given to the government.[39]

---

38 Even though the Pakistani government is not known for a lack of trying to whitewash its actions and to misinform—particularly about the PTM—the cited figures are also confirmed by activists on the ground.

39 As reported in a field interview with Interviewee 4.

The PTM's successes have inspired other ethnic minority movements, including the Missing Persons Movements in the Sindh and Balochistan provinces. A PTM leader in Swat shares, "Even some Sindhi missing persons have returned because we called for all movements of missing persons to our jalsas. They also held protests and marches in Islamabad and Sindh, and we supported them."[40]

Finally, the PTM has been successful in communicating the experiences of the tribal Pashtuns to the media and the international community. Before the movement began, the only information about the war and terrorism in the tribal areas was the official version released by the government. The PTM's resistance has opened these conflict areas to the world. Through social media posts, the PTM has criticized the Taliban's presence, documented Taliban attacks on activists (Sayeed 2019), and put pressure on the major actors to end violent extremism, terrorist attacks, and the proxy war in the Pashtun region (Express Tribune 2018). These efforts have also helped to fight the state's portrayal of the tribal Pashtuns as violent jihadis.

---

40   Interview with Interviewee 5, September 10, 2018.

Key Takeaways from the PTM for Successful Nonviolent Resistance

Mobilizing Ordinary People

The PTM has engaged ordinary people from all walks of life, including farmers, laborers, elders, women, and children. This is an effective strategy to keep the movement locally led and locally supported. This engagement fostered the local ownership of the movement which resulted in local people generously supporting the PTM in finances, logistics, and communication. At PTM events, ordinary women, men, children, and youth participate in high numbers to express their grievances, demand information about their missing relatives, and demand compensation for the destruction of their homes by the military.

Funding Campaigns Locally

The PTM's success shows the benefits of nonviolent campaigns being locally funded. This strategy can counter an adversary's claim that a campaign is supported by foreign actors to harm the state. Locally-funded campaigns can also reduce the chances of being neutralized financially by the regime.

Engaging Local Elites

Nonviolent movements can weaken the power base of an adversary by making alliances with local elite through agreements and covenants. In Pakistan, the local elite shares the political and economic power with the regime and can act as a buffer between the movement and its stronger adversary. Although tribal maliks disagreed with the PTM on the issues of enforced disappearances and local Peace Committees, they were initially open to supporting the movement. This helped PTM leaders to identify shared causes—including clearing land mines, ending targeted killings, and demanding the state media ceases depicting tribal Pashtuns as violent—and may have mitigated the severity of repression from the state in some instances.

Working with Faith Leaders

Nonviolent campaigns benefit from engaging a large number of diverse faith leaders. The PTM has utilized faith leaders to preach religiously inspired peace, human rights, nonviolent ideology, and the effectiveness of nonviolent actions. Bacha Khan promoted nonviolent jihad—drawing the concept from Islamic teachings on *jihad-i-akbar* ("the greater struggle")—which influenced Muslim (and even Hindu and Sikh) religious figures against colonial repression. By framing their movement as a spiritual successor to the Red Shirt Movement, the PTM has engaged a faith-based framework.

Building on Local Civil Resistance Legacies

As noted above, the PTM builds on the legacy of Bacha Khan and the Red Shirt Movement. Nonviolent movements can draw inspiration from local knowledge of a region's historical practice of nonviolent resistance. This can be a significant factor in strengthening unity and developing effective communication strategies that appeal to the shared history, experiences, and understanding among the local population. It can also strengthen a movement's resolve to maintain nonviolent discipline, as it juxtaposes its own nonviolent organizing with the successful nonviolent actions of its progenitors.

Reinforcing Nonviolent Discipline

A movement's leadership plays an important role in maintaining nonviolent discipline in its interactions with a violent opponent. The PTM's clear messages of commitment to remain nonviolent by key leaders have built up the movement's moral strength. This commitment can also reduce the severity and frequency of state repression. In a country where violent protests are common, nonviolent actions are deeply appreciated by neutral members of society. Manzoor Pashteen frequently reminds his supporters about his commitment to the use of nonviolent strategies and tactics, despite severe repression from Pakistan's security forces.

Inclusion of Women in Leadership Roles

Nonviolent campaigns should be inclusive of women of all ages, since women's leadership and participation broaden a movement's representation of the general public. Greater representation can increase a movement's effectiveness while also politically empowering a traditionally repressed group. This is particularly important in Pakistan's patriarchal society. One of the most significant impacts of the PTM is the increased participation of women in society through the movement's actions and through electoral processes in the newly represented tribal areas of Pakistan. This trend is important to sustain and multiply.

Representing Multiple Ethnic Groups

Nonviolent movements should be inclusive of other suppressed groups in order to build effective people power rather than only focus on one in-group identity. The PTM's actions revolve around Pashtun identity, as is evident from its name and slogans. The PTM has however reached out to other ethnic groups, including expressing solidarity with Baloch and Sindhi women and through developing communication strategies that emphasize common grievances such as enforced disappearances, targeted killings, and militant attacks on ethnic and religious minorities. Movements are stronger when they are able to build inter-ethnic unity and develop tangible solidarity actions with and outreach to other repressed minority groups to reduce ethnic, racial, linguistic, and social divisions.

Balanced Use of Social Media

Nonviolent movements can secure external support and build internal unity through the strategic but balanced use of social media. The PTM has deployed social media as their main communication tool, and, as such, the effectiveness of their online activities has largely depended on Facebook, Twitter, and WhatsApp. An overreliance on social media can undermine mobilization for the movement, since many potential supporters of the PTM do not have internet access or are illiterate. The state can also shut down or slow down the internet, which would harm online organizing. However, the PTM has demonstrated that it is capable of balancing and diversifying its online tactical repertoire with on-the-ground organizing and offline communication to accommodate for internet disruptions. Offline communications include visits to public places such as shopping centers, bazaars, and bus stations. During these visits, PTM activists communicate their grievances to the public through handbills and pamphlets, and through verbal communication with illiterate persons. These varied tactics of communication have been a successful strategy of resistance for the PTM.

The findings of this report suggest that the inclusion of indigenous knowledge, diverse actors and supporters, and global means of seeking justice is key in making a nonviolent movement an effective and powerful catalyst for change in society. The PTM movement demonstrates that nonviolent civil resistance can be an impactful and successful strategy in a society where violence and ruthless suppression is the norm.

Appendix I: The Terror Networks, the War on Terror, and Their Effects on Tribal Pashtuns

"If Taliban safe havens are eliminated from Pakistan, particularly from FATA, and the Pakistani state discards the 'good and bad Taliban' policy, the Pashtuns in Afghanistan will heave a sigh of relief." – Manzoor Pashteen, interview with DW News, *April 11, 2018*

There is a complex network of terrorist groups and organizations in the tribal areas of Pakistan. These groups include Al-Qaeda, the Taliban, and *Lashkar-e-Jhangvi Al-Alami*, or the "Army of Jhangvi International." The *Lashkar-e-Jhangvi Al-Alami* is an anti-Shia terrorist group—an offshoot of *Sipah-i-Sahaba Pakistan*, or the "Guardians of the Prophet's Companions"—that perpetrates terrorist attacks on the Shias of Afghanistan by infiltrating the country from Pakistan's tribal areas. The militants in these groups include Afghans, Arabs, Chechens, Uzbeks, Tajiks, local Pashtuns, and other Pakistani ethnic and sectarian groups.

The Taliban can be further categorized into Afghan Taliban and the *Tehrik-i-Taliban Pakistan* (TTP), or the "Taliban Movement in Pakistan." Afghan Taliban, including the Haqqani Network which mainly operates in Afghanistan, are pro-Pakistan and are referred to by the Pakistani authorities as the "Good Taliban" or Mujahideen. The TTP is referred to by the Pakistani authorities as the "Bad Taliban." This report refers to all of the groups mentioned above interchangeably as militants, extremists, or terrorists. The PTM is against all of these groups and wants to remove them from the Pashtun territory.

The state and its foreign allies launched several operations in the tribal areas as part of the War on Terror campaign. Operation *Rah-e-Nijat*, or "Path to Salvation," began in June 2009 with Pakistan's security forces aiming to expel the TTP and their allies from South Waziristan. To flush out the militants from the area, the entire civilian population of SW was relocated. More than 107,000 families, mainly from the Mehsud tribe, became internally displaced persons (IDPs) in the first seven months following the start of the operation (Khan 2012). Some moved to the nearby IDP camps in the districts of Tank and Banu of the KP province while others migrated to larger cities in the region such as Peshawar, Rawalpindi, and Karachi.

Pashtun IDPs have faced difficulty finding new places to live due to the state's narrative that labeled Pashtuns as terrorists. In 2014, the provincial governments of Punjab and Sindh banned the entry of tribal Pashtun IDPs into their territories. They claimed that the Taliban would infiltrate their provinces by hiding among tribal civilians. In another case of

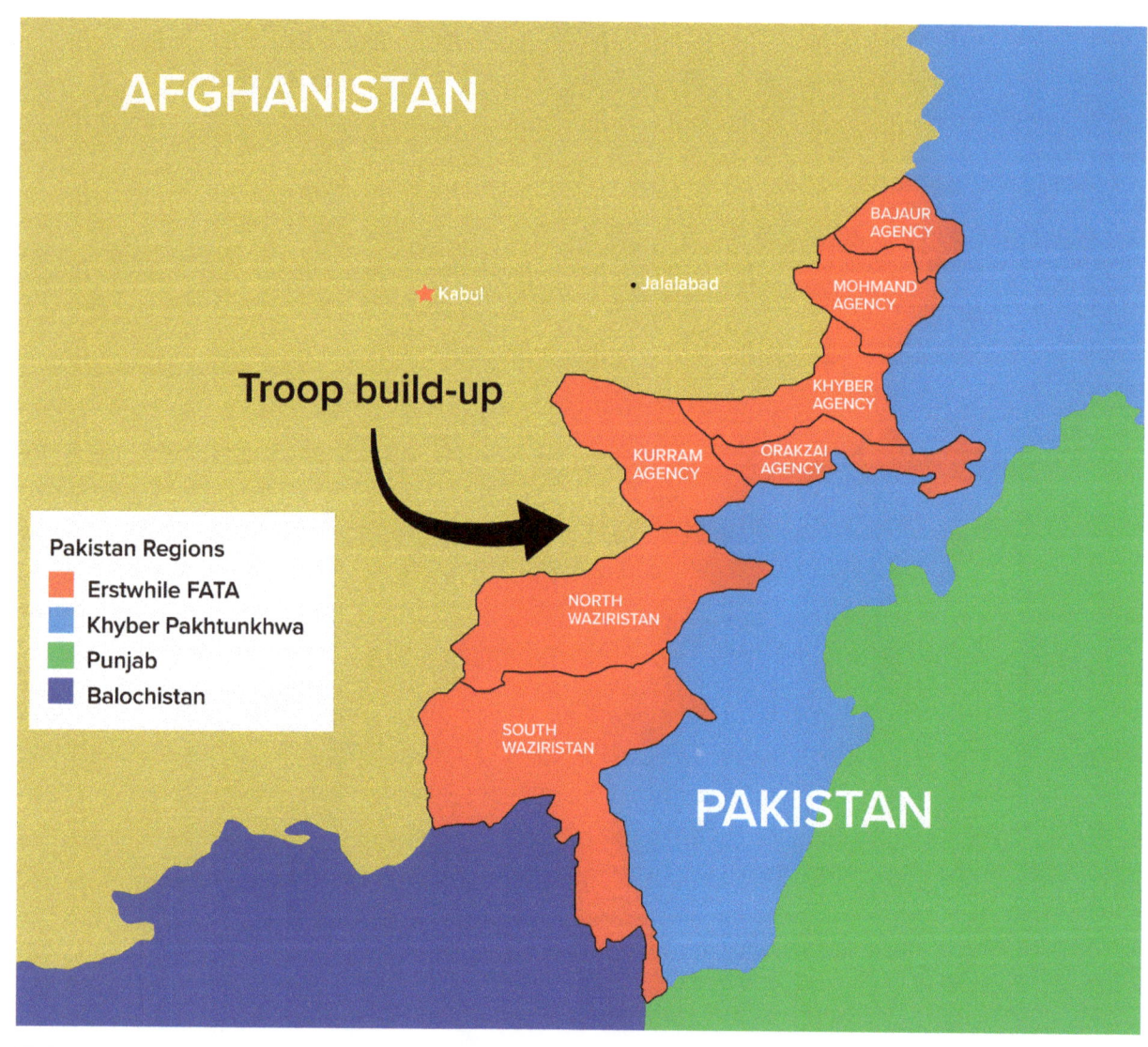

MAP 2. The Seven Former FATA Regions on the Pakistan–Afghanistan Border

This map indicates the strategic location of the former seven FATA regions near the border of Pakistan and Afghanistan. Military offenses in North Waziristan and South Waziristan led to the dislocation of the entire population in these regions, mostly to the neighboring districts of Banu and Tank.

state-instigated racism, security forces in the regions of Punjab and Islamabad arrested hundreds of Pashtun laborers, shopkeepers, and hawkers as part of the counterterrorism operations in 2017 (Siddiqui 2019).

On April 10, 2010, Pakistani fighter jets bombed targets in Sra Vela, a village in the Khyber district, believing they were striking a meeting attended by a high-level militant commander.

Instead, they hit the home of a pro-government family whose three brothers were serving in government forces. A second bomb hit a group of neighbors while they were trying to help those injured in the first strike. At least 60 civilians were killed and 30 injured. Civilians were also killed in the crossfire between the militants and the military.

Despite ongoing military operations, in 2010, security forces declared South Waziristan safe for the repatriation of IDPs. Four years later, in June 2014, the Pakistani military launched Operation *Zarb-e-Azab*, or "sharp and cutting strike," in neighboring North Waziristan (NW) that led to the largest internal displacement in the country's history. Within the first month of the operation close to a million civilians, from 80,302 families, were reported by the Pakistani authorities to be displaced. In the summer of 2018, more than 14,000 families were still awaiting government permission and assistance to return to NW. By December 2019, these figures had decreased to 2,000 families remaining in the Baka-Khel IDP Camp.

When the IDPs began returning to their homes, in addition to other daily hardships, they encountered land mines laid by the military during its operation against militants. According to the PTM, 77 people had been wounded and at least 18 killed by land mines as of February 2018. In the erstwhile FATA, the army and militants used land mines, such as improvised explosive devices (IEDs), as an offensive weapon—strewn inside school buildings, homes, and in agricultural fields. Most of the victims of land mines were children and women. From March 2000 to July 2019, there were 498 landmine explosions in Pakistan. These explosions have led to 1,026 dead and 2,447 injured persons. The greatest number of landmine deaths and injuries were reported in the erstwhile FATA (172), followed by KP (132), Balochistan (83), Sindh (70), and Punjab (45). The highest number of fatalities from land mines, 371, were reported in the erstwhile FATA (SATP 2019).

The military operations in the tribal areas also led to enforced disappearances. The Commission of Inquiry on Enforced Disappearances (CIED) has handled more than 4,000 cases since its inception in 2011, but to date not one perpetrator of the enforced disappearances has been brought to justice. However, according to human rights organizations and activists, the number of missing persons is much higher than the CIED's caseload. According to Manzoor Pashteen, since the start of the military operations in the Pashtun region more than 30,000 Pashtuns in the region have gone missing.

Appendix II: A Note on the Interview Subjects

Six key leaders and activists from the Pashtun Protection Movement took part in interviewees with the author for this study. For safety concerns, their names have been withheld in this publication. In Table 2, descriptions of each of the interview participants are provided.

TABLE 2: INTERVIEWEES FOR THIS STUDY	
INTERVIEW SUBJECT	DESCRIPTION
Interviewee 1	Male activist and PTM leader from District Tank
Interviewee 2	Male university student and PTM activist from Peshawar city
Interviewee 3	Woman leader and PTM activist from Islamabad
Interviewee 4	Male activist and PTM coordinator from Denmark
Interviewee 5	Woman educator and PTM leader from District Swat
Interviewee 6	Male PTM activist from Islamabad

CITED BIBLIOGRAPHY

Banerjee, Mukulika. *The Pathan Unarmed: Opposition & Memory in the North West Frontier*. Santa Fe: School of American Research Press, 2000.

Banting, Erinn. *Afghanistan: The People.* New York: Crabtree Publishing Company, 2003.

Bukhari, Sharmeen. 2020. "In the Pictures is Sagar Mukesh Meghwar...." *Facebook*, January 20, 2021. https://www.facebook.com/sharmeen.bukhari.146/posts/839784470209986.

Center for Research & Security Studies Islamabad [CRSSI]. *Annual Security Report – 2019 (Press Release)*. December 30, 2019. https://crss.pk/story/31-reduction-in-terrorism-in-2019-improving-security-situation-reports-crss/.

Daily Times. "Twitterati React to Punjab Govt's Muharram Ad Featuring Manzoor Pashteen." September 15, 2018. https://dailytimes.com.pk/298517/twitterati-react-to-punjab-govts-muharram-ad-featuring-manzoor-pashteen-2/.

Dawar, Mohsin. "I Want to Thank..." *Twitter*, February 5, 2021. https://twitter.com/mjdawar/status/1357641569743101954.

Ejaz, Sanna. 2021. "I Just Reached Home!" *Facebook*, January 17, 2021. https://www.facebook.com/sanamdn/posts/4326746194018472.

Express Tribune. "Islamabad, Army Backs US Peace Talks with Taliban." December 6, 2018. https://tribune.com.pk/story/1861478/1-army-focused-improving-reltions-idiadg-ispr/.

"Frontier Crimes Regulation." *Wikipedia*. Accessed February 22, 2019. https://en.wikipedia.org/wiki/Frontier_Crimes_Regulation.

Gandhara: Center for Peace & Culture Education. *Facebook*. Retrieved January 8, 2020. https://www.facebook.com/Gandhara-Center-for-Peace-Culture-Education-175558732644698/.

Gunaratna, Rohan, and Anders Nielsen. "Al Qaeda in the Tribal Areas of Pakistan and Beyond." *Studies in Conflict & Terrorism* 31, no. 9 (2008): 775–807.

ISPR Official [YouTube user]. "DG ISPR Press Conference." YouTube Video. April 29, 2019. https://www.youtube.com/watch?v=xIOhjM-9PaAE.

Kazam, Mohammad. "Sanna Ejaz: PTM Leader Deported to Balochistan," *BBC News*. January 18, 2021. https://www.bbc.com/urdu/pakistan-55699225.

Khan, Abdul Karim. "The Khudai Khidmatgar (Servants of God): Red Shirt Movement in the North-West Frontier Province of British India 1927–1947." PhD diss. University of Hawaii, 1997.

Khan, Adnan. "The Pashtun Tahafuz (Protection) Movement (PTM): A Threat to the Regime." *The International Marxist Tendency,* April 25, 2018. https://marxist.dk/in-english/5847-the-pashtun-tahafuz-protection-movement-ptm-a-threat-to-the-regime.html.

Khan, Aina. "How a Pakistani Folk Band Changed Pashtun Narrative Through Music," *Al Jazeera*. January 21, 2021. https://www.aljazeera.com/news/2021/1/21/folk-music-more-to-pashtuns-beyond-extremism.

Khan, Zahid Ali. "Military Operations in FATA and PATA: Implications for Pakistan." *Strategic Studies* 31/32, no. 1 (Spring 2012): 129–146.

Masood, Salman, Mujib Mashal, and Zia ur-Rehman. "Time Is Up: Pakistan's Army Targets Protest Movement, Stifling Dissent." *New York Times*, May 28, 2019. https://www.nytimes.com/2019/05/28/world/asia/pakistan-pashtun-dissent.html.

Mehsud, Sailab. "Wana Market Dynamited as Punishment for Major's Killing." *Dawn News*, November 5, 2016. https://www.dawn.com/news/1294376/wana-market-dynamited-as-punishment-for-majors-killing.

Naya Daur. "Management of Tribal Areas Should Be Handed Over to Civilians: Waziristan Peace Jirga Demands," February 5, 2021. https://urdu.nayadaur.tv/55096/.

Pakistan Tahafuz Movement Official [PTMO]. *Facebook.* Retrieved 2020. https://www.facebook.com/groups/729081397428482.

Pashteen, Manzoor Ahmad. 2020. "Meeting with the Leaders of the Forum for Raising Voices for Missing Persons in Sindh." *Facebook*, December 5, 2020. https://www.facebook.com/manzoor.mehsud/posts/3465053163592370.

Pashtun Global Diaspora. *Facebook.* Retrieved September 16, 2019. https://www.facebook.com/pashtungd.

"Pashtun Tahafuz Movement." *Wikipedia.* Last modified August 21, 2021. https://en.wikipedia.org/wiki/Pashtun_Tahafuz_Movement.

Pashtun Tahafuz Movement Official (PTMO). *Facebook.* https://www.facebook.com/groups/729081397428482.

Power TV Talk Shows [YouTube user]. "Mohsin Dawar Speech in National Assembly Today." YouTube Video. October 1, 2019. https://www.youtube.com/watch?v=SdUj3ZQXBNA.

Roggio, Bill. "Taliban Capture 25 Pakistani Security Personnel in Swat." *Foundation for Defense of Democracies' Long War Journal*, July 29, 2008. https://www.fdd.org/analysis/2008/07/29/taliban-capture-25-pakistani-security-personnel-in-swat/.

Sayeed, Saad. "Pakistan Activists' Arrests Fuel Tension with Afghanistan." *Reuters*, February 7, 2019. https://www.reuters.com/article/us-pakistan-arrests/pakistan-activists-arrests-fuel-tension-with-afghanistan-idUSKCN1PW0XS.

Sayers, Eric. "The Islamic Emirate of Waziristan and the Bajaur Tribal Region: The Strategic Threat of Terrorist Sanctuaries." *Center for Security Policy*, February 16, 2007. https://centerforsecuritypolicy.org/the-islamic-emirate-of-waziristan-and-the-bajaur-tribal-region-the-strategic-threat-of-terrorist-sanctuaries/.

Siddiqui, Zuha. "Firebranding the Frontier: The Women of the Pashtun Tahaffuz Movement." *Jamoor*, May 6, 2019. https://www.jamhoor.org/read/2019/5/06/firebranding-the-frontier-the-women-of-the-pashtun-tahaffuz-movement.

South Asia Terrorism Portal [SATP]. 2019. https://www.satp.org/.

Syed, Baqir Sajjad, and Syed Irfan Raza. "Foreign Spy Agencies Fund PTM, Says Army." *Dawn News*, April 30, 2019. https://www.dawn.com/news/1479321.

THE CLICK PLUS [YouTube User]. "Manzoor Pashteen Speech in DI Khan Jalsa." YouTube Video. July 15, 2018. https://www.youtube.com/watch?v=0ar7w0DLB0E.

Wazir, Ali. "Sacrifices and Struggle." *Asian Marxist Review*, May 28, 2019. http://www.marxistreview.asia/sacrifices-and-struggle-2.

Yousaf, Farooq. "Pakistan's Colonial Legacy: FCR and Postcolonial Governance in the Pashtun Tribal Frontier." *Interventions* 21, no. 2 (2019): 172–187.

IMAGE CREDITS

Figures 1, 3, 6, 7, 9, 10: Provided to the author by anonymous PTM member. Used with permission.

Figure 2: Twitter account of the PTM, @PashtunTM_Offi.

Figure 4: Twitter account of Tariq, @afghan_tariq.

Figure 5: Twitter account of Sanna Ejaz @sanaejaz2.

Figure 8: Facebook account of Mohsin Dawar, https://www.facebook.com/mohsindawar.

Figure 11: Twitter account of Manzoor Pashteen, @manzoorpashteen.

Map 1: Designed by Qamar Jafri and Bruce Pearson. Based on "Free Pakistan SVG Map" by simplemaps. Licensed under the SVG Map Library License: https://simplemaps.com/resources/svg-license.

Map 2: Designed by Qamar Jafri and Bruce Pearson. Based on Map 1 files and "NWFP FATA.svg" designed by Pahari Sahib. https://commons.wikimedia.org/w/index.php?curid=2211738. Licensed under Creative Commons Attribution-ShareAlike 3.0 Unported (CC BY-SA 3.0): https://creativecommons.org/licenses/by-sa/3.0/.

ACKNOWLEDGMENTS

I, the author, would like to acknowledge the extensive support and critical feedback provided by Dr. Steve Chase and Dr. Maciej Bartkowski in completing this project. I would also like to thank Bruce Pearson, Julia Constantine, and Aaron Troia for providing possible lines of inquiry regarding the broad content and design of this publication. I acknowledge my anonymous contacts who helped me in connecting with the interviewees and sharing photos from the tribal areas—in particular, those interviewees who, despite facing frequent curfews and internet disconnection, traveled several kilometers from those areas to nearby internet accessible areas to record and send me their insights via audio messages. Because of this difficulty, it would take several days to complete one interview. The Expert Editor Australia provided proofreading and editing services for this publication.

About the Author

Dr. Qamar Jafri holds a PhD in Sociology from the Social and Global Studies Centre of RMIT University Australia. His research interests include identity, youth, political violence, peacebuilding, and nonviolent civil resistance. Qamar's recent publications include a book chapter on digital peace activism in South Asia, a journal article on causes of violent extremism in higher education institutions of Pakistan, and a blog article on political conflict and digital feminism in Pakistan. He has received a policy brief award from Toda Peace Institute Japan, a fellowship on nonviolent civil resistance from ICNC, a peace grant from Lisle International, and an International Postgraduate Research Scholarship from RMIT. He obtained MS in Sociology from International Islamic University Islamabad.

www.ingramcontent.com/pod-product-compliance
Lightning Source LLC
Chambersburg PA
CBHW051405110526
44592CB00023B/2961